We are grateful for our past, present and future students who have made outstanding contributions to make our program successful for the past few decades. We understand that your journey has and will continue to be challenging, however with hard work and passion you are able to achieve great things in life.

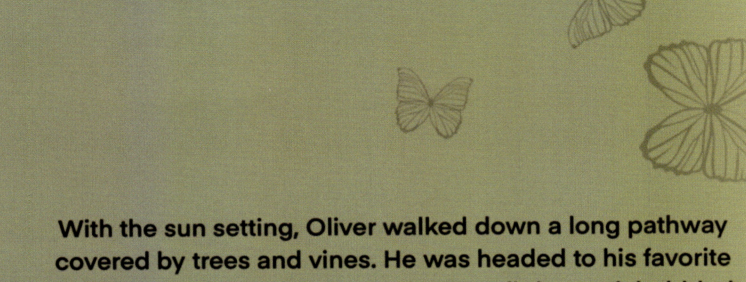

With the sun setting, Oliver walked down a long pathway covered by trees and vines. He was headed to his favorite little hideaway spot in the rainforest. A little creek babbled nearby. Oliver could hear all the familiar sounds that the forest seemed to keep as its own little secret, apart from the rest of the world. He felt safe here—no one to make fun of him or criticize him.

Oliver was particularly sad this day. He had been unable to read a portion of a book out loud in school. As he leaned over to see his reflection in the creek, he heard a whooshing sound, and from high up in the trees, a little creature came wisping down. Oliver was eye to eye with what seemed to be a tiny lemur, but one he had never seen. "Eek!" he shrieked. "Eek!" the animal shrieked back.

This little animal was different and unique like him, he thought. Although Oliver was quite a handsome little boy, he knew he was different from other children his age. He was late to talk, would mix up words with similar sounds, had a hard time naming letters, numbers, and colors, and had a difficult time reading and spelling.

"Well, hello there. My name is Eloise," spoke the little animal. "I am an aye-aye, the most different kind of lemur."
"Hello, I am Oliver," he stated in a timid voice. "I am dyslexic, a different kind of learner."
"Don't we make a pair? Both different and unique—pretty special in our own way, I'd say," said Eloise. "Tee hee I made a rhyme, in no time!"

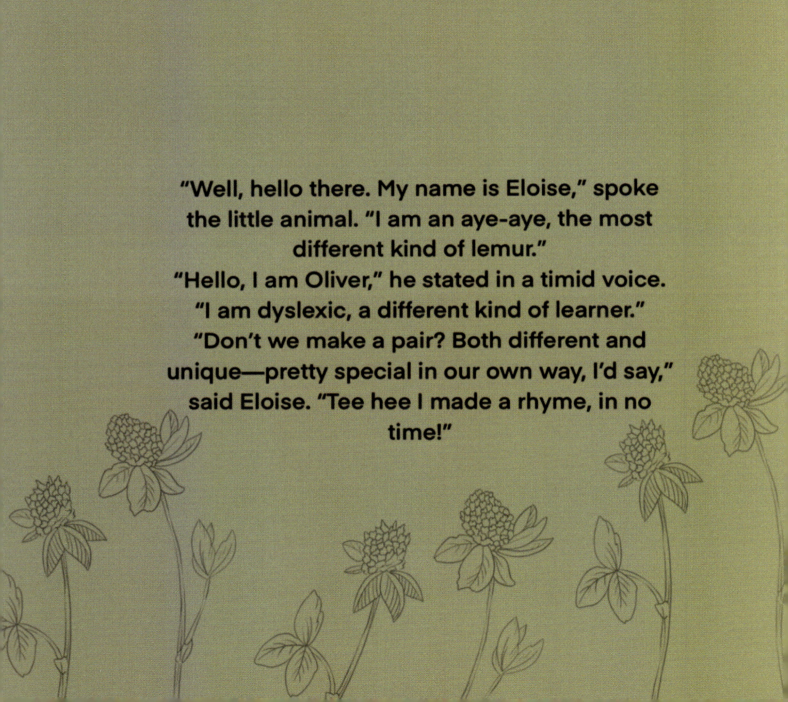

"I have a hard time with rhymes," sighed Oliver.
"That's okay," smiled Eloise. "I have a difficult time finding food, but my extra-long fingers help me," Eloise said while tapping on a nearby tree root.
"I also have to live in the treetops, but I have a fear of heights," winced Eloise.

After a long time and much conversation had passed, Oliver realized that it was time to go home. Reluctantly, he said, "Good night." As he wandered home, the pathway lit by the moon's bright glow, Oliver thought about Eloise and his differences and difficulties, and wished upon a star that he could use his own differences to work for him instead of against. Perhaps then, school would be easier.

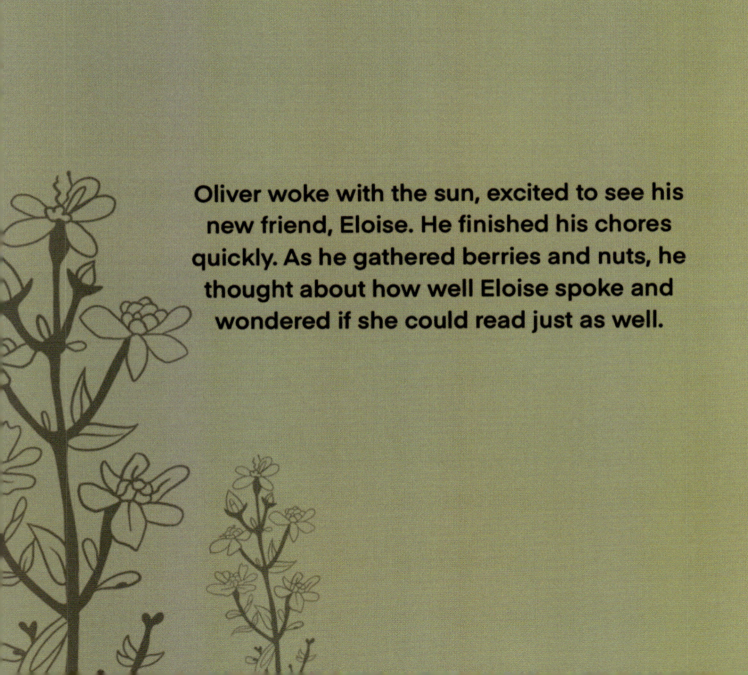

Oliver woke with the sun, excited to see his new friend, Eloise. He finished his chores quickly. As he gathered berries and nuts, he thought about how well Eloise spoke and wondered if she could read just as well.

As the sunlight traveled away, Oliver scooped up some of the fruits and nuts he had gathered and his book, which he didn't much like. It was hard for him to sound out unfamiliar words, making it difficult to read. At dusk, the book in hand, he ran down the path to find Eloise. As he reached his special spot, he cried out, "Eloise, come out—come out, wherever you are!"

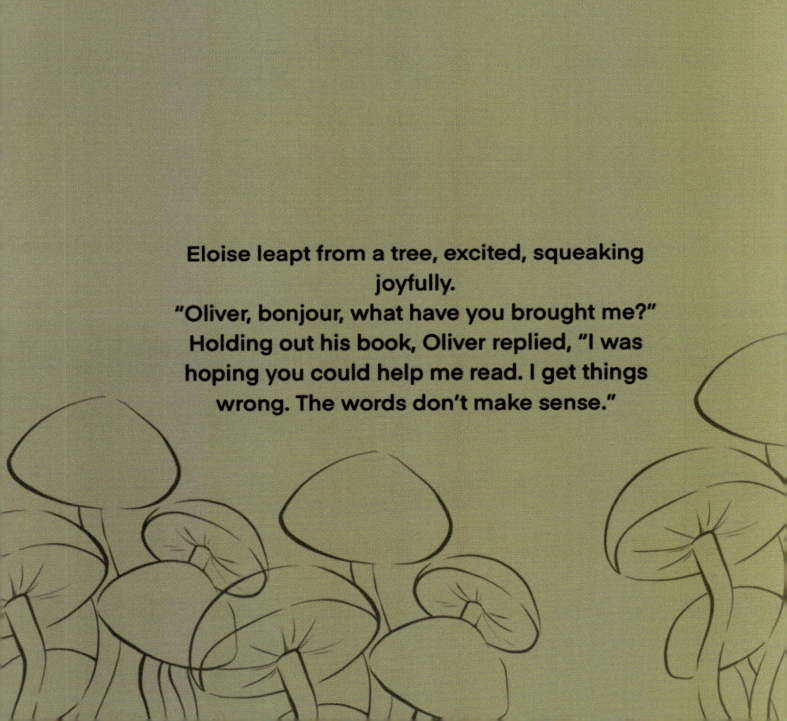

Eloise leapt from a tree, excited, squeaking joyfully.
"Oliver, bonjour, what have you brought me?"
Holding out his book, Oliver replied, "I was hoping you could help me read. I get things wrong. The words don't make sense."

Eloise replied, "It's okay—making mistakes means you are trying."

"But I read so slow," Oliver replied.

Eloise smiled and shrugged her shoulders, saying, "If you read slow, you are just creating anticipation. Let us start from the beginning, sounding out each word. It will take you a bit to learn to do this. Do not get frustrated—just keep going, and one day it will come more naturally, but only with practice."

Eloise gently patted Oliver on the head and stated, "Sometimes, taking one tiny step is better than taking no step at all."

Night after night, Oliver and Eloise met at their special, safe place in the jungle, under the moonlit sky, to read together.
"You provided strength to me when I thought I had none. I CAN read!" exclaimed Oliver.

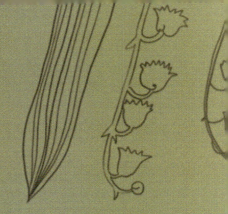

"Yes, you can!" Eloise said with great pride. "Never worry; life is like our little creek. There are many obstacles to overcome, but you will get to where you want, with your own strength and knowledge," Eloise grinned with great satisfaction.

A beautiful friendship was formed. Oliver and Eloise now have a better understanding that differences can also be strengths. Eek, how wonderful.

Is My Child Dyslexic?
(Academic Language Therapy Association (ALTA), 2019)

What is Dyslexia?

Dyslexia is a neurological condition that impairs a person's ability to process written language, which affects areas such as reading and writing. The severity of dyslexia may vary greatly from none person to another. Without effective intervention, the daily challenges caused by dyslexia become more complex and difficult over time.

Early Warning Signs and Symptoms

A child with dyslexia may exhibit signs ranging from difficulty rhyming, confusing the order of letters in words they are reading, trouble making sense of the words they read, and/or difficulty mastering spelling assignments. The signs that point to dyslexia change over time as a child ages. Early warning signs in preschool children often include some of the following:

- Delayed speech
- Difficulty pronouncing words correctly
- Difficulty learning the names of letters, numbers, colors, or shapes
- Difficulty following directions

Symptoms of dyslexia in school-aged children may include some or all of the following:

- Persistent difficulty in areas mentioned above
- Reading very slowly, difficulty reading aloud, or reading well below the expected level
- Mispronouncing words, an inability to sound out words, or difficulty finding the right word
- Persistently poor and inconsistent spelling
- Problems processing, understanding, or summarizing what is read or heard
- Avoidance of activities that involve reading and/or writing
- Anxiety about going to school (e.g., stomachaches, tearfulness, headaches)
- After school "meltdowns" (e.g., anger, tears, tantrums), particularly when doing homework assignments that involve reading/writing

Without effective treatment, dyslexia can lead to a number of serious issues. Children with dyslexia often can't keep up with their peers in academic skills, which can lead to low self-esteem, anxiety, and intense frustration.

If parents suspect dyslexia, it's important to support children with patience and encouragement, while engaging experts who can provide the proper screening or evaluation, and diagnosis if positive identification is made. Dyslexic learners then need a period of specialized instruction by a skilled professional such as a Certified Academic Language Practitioner for tutoring, or a Licensed Academic Language Therapist when more intensive intervention is recommended.

Academic Language Therapy Association 2019, Academic Language Therapy Association (ALTA) website, accessed 28 October 2023, <http://www.altaread.org>.